Investigate

Landforms

Jane Penrose

Heinemann Library
Chicago, Illinois

www.capstonepub.com
Visit our website to find out more information about Heinemann-Raintree books.

To order:
☎ Phone 800-747-4992
💻 Visit www.capstonepub.com to browse our catalog and order online.

Edited by Siân Smith, Rebecca Rissman, and Charlotte Guillain
Designed by Joanna Hinton-Malivoire
Original illustrations © Capstone Global Library
Picture research by Elizabeth Alexander and Sally Cole
Originated by Modern Age Repro House Ltd
Printed and bound in the United States of America in Eau Claire, Wisconsin. 080414   008417R

14 13
10 9 8 7 6 5 4 3

Library of Congress Cataloging-in-Publication Data
Penrose, Jane.
  Landforms / Jane Penrose.
    p. cm. – (Investigate geography)
  Includes bibliographical references and index.
  ISBN 978-1-4329-3469-9 (hc) – ISBN 978-1-4329-3477-4 (pb) 1.
Landforms–Juvenile literature. I. Title.
  GB406.P43 2009
  551.41–dc22
                    2009011041

Acknowledgments
The author and publishers are grateful to the following for permission to reproduce copyright material: Alamy pp. **12** (© South West Images Scotland), **20** (© Javier Etcheverry), **29** (© Brandon Cole Marine Photography); Corbis pp. **9** (© Jose Fuste Raga), **10** (© Kenji Kondo/EPA), **17** (© WEDA/EPA), **19** (© Danny Lehman), **21** (© Jeff Topping), **25** (© Craig Lovell); iStockphoto pp. **23 top left** (© Mark Kostich), **23 bottom right**, **23 bottom left** (© Alain Couillaud), **23 top right** (© Eileen Hart); Photolibrary pp. **4** (Chad Ehlers/Nordic Photos), **5** (Image100), **6** (Martin Rugner/ Age Fotostock), **7** (Peter Adams/Digital Vision), **14 & 15** (Andoni Canela/Age Fotostock), **22** (Dinodia/Age Fotostock), **24** (John Warburton-Lee Photography), **26** (Carini Joe/Pacific Stock), **27** (Andoni Canela/Age Fotostock); Shutterstock p. **13** (© Briedis).

Cover photograph of Blasket Islands, Ireland, reproduced with permission of Corbis/© The Irish Image Collection.

Every effort has been made to contact copyright holders of material reproduced in this book. Any omissions will be rectified in subsequent printings if notice is given to the publishers.

Contents

What Are Landforms? 4

Changing Landforms. 6

Mountains 8

Hills 12

Volcanoes 14

Valleys 18

Plateaus and Plains 22

Islands 26

Checklist 30

Glossary 31

Index 32

Some words are shown in bold, **like this**. You can find out what they mean by looking in the glossary.

What Are Landforms?

Earth is made up of different kinds of land. Some land is high, such as mountains. Some land is low, such as valleys.

⬆ Different landforms make our world very beautiful.

The different shapes of land you see are called landforms. Some landforms look beautiful, while others look very strange.

⬆ The Heart Reef is a **coral** island in Australia naturally shaped like a heart.

Changing Landforms

Different landforms are made in different ways. Most landforms are made by nature. Many change shape because of **erosion**.

⬇ Wind blew away the soil and sand, leaving these strange stone towers in Western Australia.

⬆ The arch called Durdle Door in Dorset, England, was made by the sea rushing in and out. One day, the sides of the arch will wear away and the arch will fall down.

Erosion is when the **surface** of Earth gets worn down, washed away, or blown away. Erosion happens all the time, all around us. It is usually caused by water or wind.

7

Mountains

Earth's **surface** is made of huge plates of rock. When these plates move, they can push against each other. This can push up the land in the middle to make mountains.

These two plates are moving toward each other. The land in the middle has been pushed up to make a mountain.

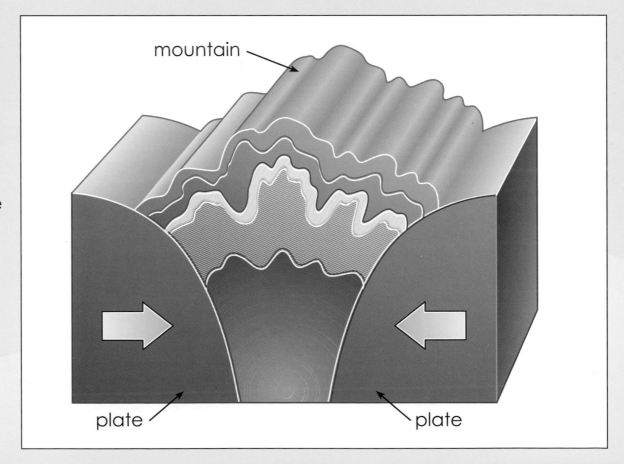

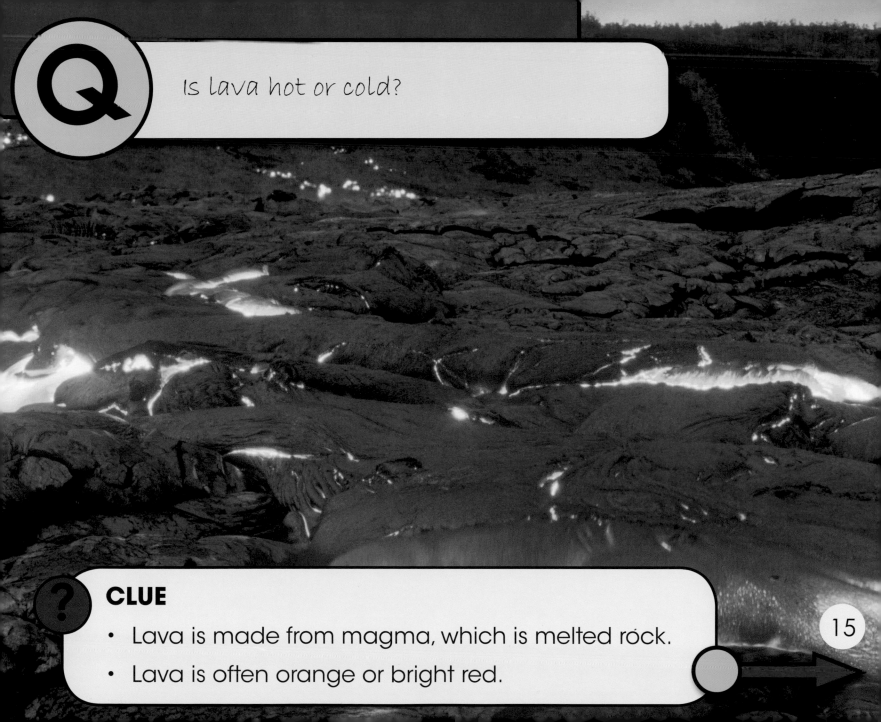

Q

Is lava hot or cold?

CLUE

- Lava is made from magma, which is melted rock.
- Lava is often orange or bright red.

15

A Lava is very, very hot. It comes from about 90 miles (150 kilometers) inside Earth. It is so hot inside Earth that rocks can melt.

When there is too much **pressure**, lava is pushed through the top of the volcano. This is an eruption.

Magma lets off gases and steam. This builds up pressure.

On May 20, 1883, Indonesia's Krakatua volcano **erupted**.

⇒ The eruption sent so much rock and ash into the air that it blocked out the Sun for days.

⇒ The noise was so loud that people heard it 1,930 miles (3,106 kilometers) away in Australia.

⇒ The eruption killed 36,417 people.

⇒ It destroyed 165 villages and towns.

➡ Many people still live near volcanoes that could erupt at any time.

Valleys

The low land between mountains and hills is called a valley. There are two types of valleys: U-shaped valleys and V-shaped valleys.

V-shaped valleys are made by rivers flowing through the land. The river water **erodes** the mountain sides, making the valley deeper and deeper.

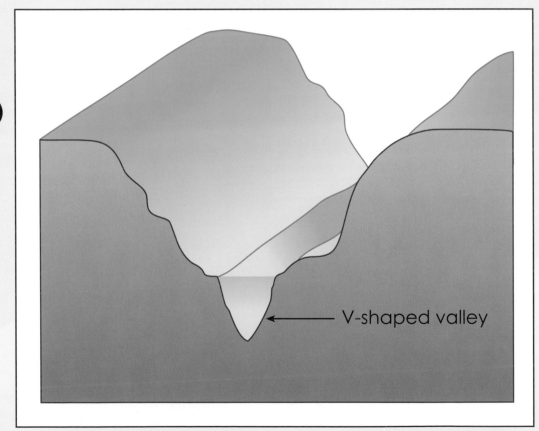

V-shaped valley

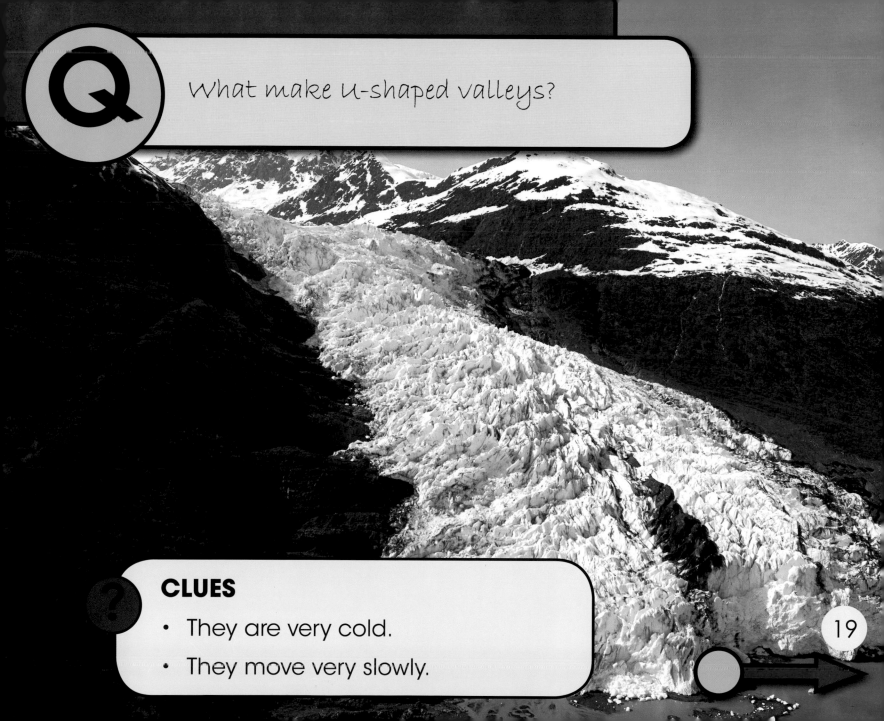

Q What make U-shaped valleys?

CLUES

- They are very cold.
- They move very slowly.

19

A U-shaped valleys are made by glaciers. They are like enormous slow rivers of snow and ice. Glaciers move down mountains, pushing and carving away the rock to make a valley.

↑ This is what a glacier looks like up close.

**A**

Many mountains have snow at the top. This is because they are so high up. The air at the top is very cold, so snow can fall.

 Mount Everest, in Nepal, is the world's tallest mountain. People who climb Everest have to wear special warm clothes and take **oxygen** to breathe.

Q What would you find on top of some mountains?

CLUES

- Is it hot or cold at the top of a mountain?
- Where do people ski?

Canyons are very deep valleys.

⇒ The Grand Canyon in Arizona is 277 miles (445 kilometers) long, up to 18 miles (29 kilometers) wide, and 5,000 feet (1,524 meters) deep.

⇒ It was made by the Colorado River **eroding** the sides of a mountain range.

⇒ The canyon started forming six million years ago.

⬆ In 2005 a glass **semicircle** bridge was made over the Grand Canyon. It lets visitors walk over the top of the canyon.

Plateaus and Plains

A plateau is a high area of land with a flat top. Some plateaus are made when the tops of mountains get worn away by **erosion**.

⬆ Some plateaus are made when large, flat areas of land get pushed up by plates moving together.

A plain is a low area of land that is very flat.

Which of these animals live on a plain?

A All of these animals live on a plain. Lots of different grasses grow on plains. This makes a plain a very good **habitat** for many different animals.

⬇ Some people go on safari on the plains of Africa. They hope to see lions, elephants, giraffes, hippos, rhinos, and many other animals.

Up to 1.5 million wildebeest can move at the same time. This is called a **migration**.

The Serengeti Plain is in Tanzania, in Africa.

➡ Many wildebeest live on the Serengeti Plain, eating the grass that grows there.

➡ The wildebeest travel 1,800 miles (2,900 kilometers) during the year, looking for fresh grass.

25

Islands

Land that is surrounded by water is called an island. Some islands are formed when the sea **erodes** bits of land away from the **mainland**. Islands can be made of rock, sand, or **coral**.

A Land is underneath an island. An island is the top part of a high piece of land, such as a hill or a mountain. The island of Hawaii would be the tallest mountain on Earth if you measured it from the bottom of the ocean floor to its top.

Some islands are the tops of volcanoes. Krakatua (see page 17) is a volcanic island.

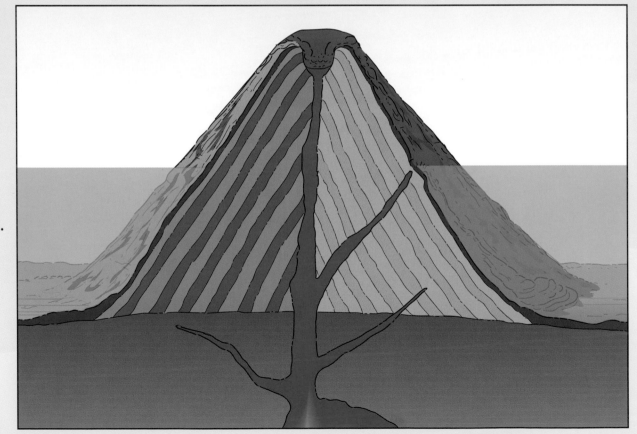

An **atoll** is an island made from **coral**. Atolls are often ring-shaped. The hole in the middle is where a rock island, usually a volcano, used to be. The volcano in the middle stopped **erupting** and **eroded** away, while the coral atoll stayed there.

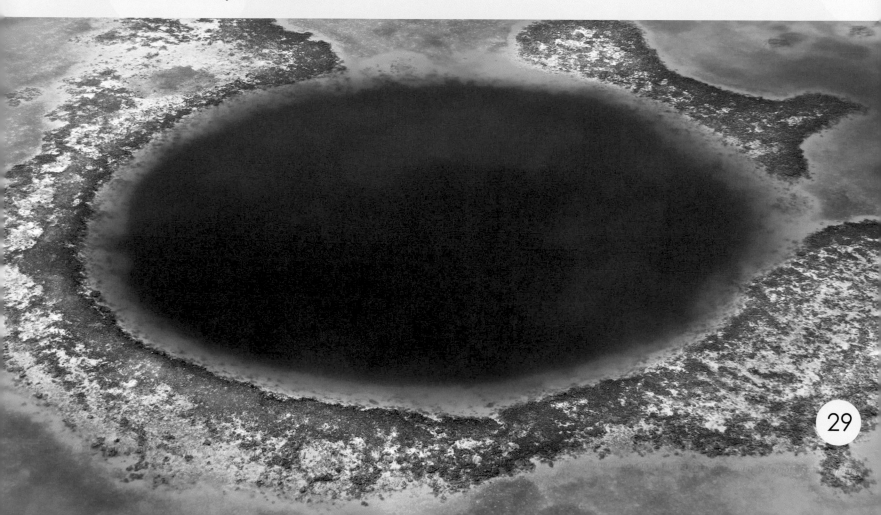

Checklist

Land on the **surface** of Earth forms many different shapes. These different shapes are called landforms.

Some of Earth's landforms are:

⇒ hills

⇒ islands

⇒ mountains

⇒ plateaus and plains

⇒ valleys

⇒ volcanoes.

Glossary

atoll island made of coral

continent one of the seven largest land areas on Earth

coral colorful rock-like material made from many millions of skeletons of sea creatures

erode wear away

erosion gradual wearing away

erupt explode

habitat somewhere that animals and plants live

mainland main part of land on the coast

migration move from one place to another

mining digging underground for things like precious metals or coal

oxygen gas in the air that people and other animals need to breathe

pressure when something is in too small a space and it pushes strongly with force against something else

semicircle half a circle

surface top area of something

Index

animals 23–25
atolls 29

canyons 21
continents 11
coral islands 5, 26, 29

erosion 6–7, 13, 18, 21,
  22, 26, 29

glaciers 13, 20

hills 12–13, 28

islands 5, 26–29

lava 14, 15, 16

magma 14, 15, 16
migration 25
mining 12
mountains 4, 8–11, 28

plains 23–25
plateaus 22

snow and ice 10, 20

valleys 4, 18–21
volcanoes 14–17, 28, 29